To Nina Lukou

With respect and friendship

Ronald E Mun

ALTERITY

ALTERITY

Poetry by Ronald E. Moore

Current
Enterprise, Oregon

Current
608 East Greenwood
Enterprise, OR 97828

www.hiatt-literary.com

www.alterityonline.com

Library of Congress Cataloging-in-Publication Data

Moore, Ronald E.
  Alterity : poetry / by Ronald E. Moore.
      p. cm.
  ISBN 0-915214-43-1 (alk. paper)
  I. Title.

  PS3613.O5668A8 2006
  811'.6—dc22

                              2006030422

Manufactured in Canada

First Printing, 2007

For my sons

and

to the one loved

PUBLISHER'S NOTE

My old friend Charles Potts said, "Poetry is the last pure art form from which you can never sell out—no one will buy it." True. Poetry is beyond the measure of money. Ron Moore knows this and offers the priceless. *Alterity* caught me and won't let me go.

> You can see the chiseling
> by opening a vein
> and watching weathered words
> tumble out.

Moore sorts through the sandbox of words and produces a Schrodinger's box of meaning.

Current co-published the first complete English translation of *Meter One of the Divan-i Kebir* of Mevlana Celaleddin Rumi with the Ministry of Culture of the Republic of Turkey. We have published the poetry of Rumi, Charles Potts, Stephen Thomas, Scott Preston, W. R. Wilkens, and are proud to add Ron Moore. Current is part of a publishing triad at: hiatt-literary.com

ARTWORK

Scott and Stuart Gentling are twin Fort Worth, Texas artists for whom the oft used title "Renaissance Men" might not be an exaggeration. Their portraits, landscapes and still life paintings hang in important collections throughout the world including the White House. Their elephant folio *Of Birds of Texas* has been described by critics as the "most magnificent book in Texas publishing history."

Another book "From Time to Time" the art of Scott and Stuart Gentling is forthcoming from the University of Texas Press. It will chronicle a wider range of their interests to include not only ornithology but history, Aztec scholarship and musee.

Scott's own love of classical music, both as performer and composer, led to the creation of "Amadeus." Stuart's mysterious watercolor study titled "Pythia" depicts a Hellenistic bronze sculpture fragmented from the Gentling's own extensive collection of ancient art.

In August of 2006, during the production of this book, Stuart Gentling died. We mourn his loss and honor his memory.

"We should try to love the questions themselves, like locked rooms and like books that are written in a very foreign tongue."

RILKE

"Art is a way of forgiving the world for its evil and chaos."

LESZEK KOLAKOWSI

"We are all drawn toward the same craters of the spirit— to know what we are and what we are for, to know our purpose, to seek grace."

SAUL BELLOW

ACKNOWLEDGMENTS

The author thanks *descant* for reprint permissions, and its editor, David Kuhne. The author expresses appreciation to Valerie Freeman, Todd Moore, Mark Moore, Stuart and Scott Gentling, Fanchee Whitaker, Mary Volcansek, and with all respect, Betsy Colquitt.

CONTENTS

EPILOGUE

PROLOGUE

MEDITATIONS ON REGRET

I am not Marco Polo.

But I have stuffed my pockets
with contraband from forty-nine countries.
Shown several faces to the world.
Been a deck of cards to myself.

And now I'm in another place
I can't speak the language of,
trying to persuade this heart,
that love is not erased, if ended.

I am the father of my errors.
What I might have done differently
would likely have been done less well.
Moments of madness did become song.

If only what survives is justified,
what chance has much of anything?
How else to redress damage done,
than by honing, the spirit– raw to the sun.

Regret that you never saw Samarkand–
not that you didn't see Paris again–
your body carries Paris within you.

I

"Philosophy begins in wonder . . . it never ends."

ROBERT NOZICK

Artist: Scott Gentling

STRING QUARTET

When I think of what I have,
and what I've let go,
the coloring and texture of
all that's flowed through me,
it's as if a string quartet is playing–
movements of phrase and variation,
dissonant melodies in search of a theme,
always drawn to the melancholy cello,
miniaturized moments of perfection,
yet when it's over–
nothing but silence hanging in air,
no evidence music was ever there, except
this sharpened sensibility.
The way the universe senses
its agonizing journey toward complexity,
a relentless auguring– particle dust to thought,
from before what's remembered,
to all that's portending.

TUTTI PAZZI

For Ken Lawrence (1935-2006)

Impossible to tell what century
you're visiting in Italy.
Lodging in the ruins of various regimes,
except the Etruscans, vanished–
destroyed by Rome for loving life too much.
One city layered on bones of the last one,
traces of smoke, sulphuric acid,
blood from long abandoned aqueducts,
the mortar of the stones, what legion
of humans torn apart, has absorbed,
the limbic system
stretching like a boot toward Sicily.
Thus, amazed,
we hear from the salt and ashes,
music of Puccini and Verdi rising,
singing a beauty sufficient for the summer sun
to pause, cry,
at the mad splendor Italy has been.

A KIND OF MARRIAGE

It's more than the touching—
the body's vernacular—
it's the seamless consonance,
a plaiting that insinuates
the entire layer of my dreams,
an integrity of wanting,
wanton in conspiracy—
who else could sense my fingers,
your breath still fresh upon them,
tapping out the rhythm of my poems
on your hip
while you sleep
after love.

DAYS OF DIFFERENTIATION

Not sameness all the time. There are days
of differentiation, from which all others
are consequence. To name them is to know
the self that was made. In the case of Dante
Alighieri– his nightmare of exile, the day he
made peace between Venice and Ravenna
merely by threatening to arrive, the night
he wrote the last terza rima of *Commedia*,
the moment, at age nine, the vision first appeared,
the object of his ineradicable love. She
blossomed in his mind as a heavenly artifact,
Beatrice, existing only in her absence,
twice removed by time. Copper of memory.
Silver of hope. Gold of imagination's fire.
Those excellent days never had. And what
beauty left on the page by the long staying,
afterward.

MEMORY

That long torrent of days,
we disappeared in the soft bed of history,
entered the light and darkness of each other.

And my penchant for refusing the possible,
practicing detachment, failing to succeed,
stubbornly protesting the lack of sufficiency.

What part of all that have I now?
The body is not made for remembering–
memory is a forger anyway–
something remaining in the spirit, the heart,
a dazzling shard, a filigree.

Something different and more than
the jacaranda leaves,
hoarding what rain they can,
until that is also taken away,
shuddering, in the wind.

WINTER IN AN EMPTY CATHEDRAL

Winter all the way into the stone,
light long departed,
climbing the stairs
of a ruined cathedral in Rouen,
the night rain cold washing over us,
the Paris trip meant to graft and fasten,
ending here, like these walls, loosening,
our ears pressed against ancient doors,
listening for a spirit we might tempt back,
whose faint voice could resurrect the heart of things,
into this once perfect building,
into the mystery of our uncoupled flesh.

TESTAMENT

Socratic philosophers have been amused
By Plato's irrational belief in *forms.*

Now we've found a nebula eighty light-years long,
Two strands of rope– one of gas, one of dust–

Magnetic forces at the center of the galaxy–
Rotating only every ten thousand years,

The ropes slowly twisting, braid around each other
In the shape of DNA– a colossal double helix.

There *are* forms, they are magnified perfection–
"Nobody has ever seen anything like this before."

Beauty is consoling, insufficiently so,
Though it overwhelms in infinite refrain.

Being is what I am a part of, uttering its name
With awe– god, the going-on of everything.

BORGES ON HIS WAY TO GENEVA

Halfway round the world he went
to walk through the shade gate,
a great horned owl in mannered flight,
his mind a castled house of books,
seven stories high and imperial.

A panoply of legends painted on its walls,
by elves who haven't lived for centuries,
changing in each manifest–
shapes, countries, languages,
exhibiting the circular illusion of time.

Calligrapher of the common
from a house of darkened eloquence,
honed words flashed across his pages,
like "The South's" blade swift in
defending gaucho honor.

From Iceland to his mother, Argentina,
he was a labyrinth of language,
repository of every tale that could be told,
his own he ended in Geneva–
the library is now closed.

I ADD YOU

to a summer afternoon,
    with the scent of bougainvillea,
    on your way to the pond where you kneel on
    the spillway as swans glide toward you,
    grace gathering.

to an autumn evening,
    amid the vacant day's shutting down,
    your nearby glass of water, your heart
    always on a mission, the recurring of your
    obvious shadow.

to winter's endless night,
    dread's long-hooded window,
    goddess of my dreams, writer of invincible
    chapters, hearing your heels pad away
    into my eternity.

POETRY AS A LAST ALTERNATIVE

Language
is insufficient,
too imprecise to say–
what an atom is or isn't,
whether it exists or doesn't,
why we must impute dark matter, or
cannot decide if light is a wave or a particle,
or whether a quark is stronger than an anti-quark,
or why quantum theory won't reconcile with gravity.
On a walk with Heisenberg,
Bohr said, "at the end
we'll have to turn to poetry."

METAPHYSICS IN THE PARK

There was little indication
that the man on the bench
was doing metaphysics in the park,
(though he knew the number
of photons in his body, 10 times 27 zeroes)
felt hat, Sunday Times,
inappropriate overcoat in spring.

He was imagining dark energy moving through his body,
whose atoms had always been somewhere,
since time began,
before being gathered in him–
in a subterranean rock on Mars,
the tail of a cheetah,
the laurel wreath Aurelius accepted, from the Mystery cults of Eleusis.

He saw in the eternal wind:
a serpentine of Russian poets, their right hands crushed,
a tablet saying: *the lies of a government are worse than a thousand broken hearts,*
a tent flap loose, dangling,
the hallowed smile of a female child,
the mouth of hell that swallowed Jews and Gypsies,
an alabaster statue of Athena.

Carrying within him these too many worlds–
carved out his loneliness,
inscribed him, a hologram, in time.

AFTER A LECTURE BY DANTE

What has ever caged me but my heart—
   a slave of rapture,
its bowstring taut, rushing forward,
   foolhardy even,
at the sight of the beautiful.

I am an otherwise, sane man,
   who has loved
to the precipice of madness,
   not for the drama or poetry,
but ungoverned necessity.

Shall I tell you how I love you?
   I am holding your hand,
sitting in a swing on the
   front porch of heaven—
bathed in pure, abundant light.

SMALL HYMN

I have climbed on six continents,
But still have not exhausted
The greedy compartments of my heart.
We all know where sorrow will go.
But I relish these ripening days–
Bestowed by dust of stars–
For what reasons
Philosophers speculate,
The rowdy throng of poets offers praise.
I wake to the everlasting rhythm,
Watching the immanent unfurl
In the inexhaustible silence of the world.

NOT WITHOUT PUCCINI

I can think of the world without me
    but not without Puccini.
Nor without that scrubbed young girl
    running to her lover
      with a heart larger than Detroit,
      with such plans, such tinseled plans,
      nails done.
And how without the olive tree, withered
    and Paris vanished,
    the jaguar stilled,
    a thousand colors gone to black.
I suppose it will come to that–
    the light disappearing from the sea.
And if, in deep time,
    it happens again,
    and someone is there to remember–
Let them praise it,
    as, in sorrow,
    I do now.

NOVALIS AND I

Love and poetry–
I've had the extravagance of each.
It must be karma and I'd like to thank,
whoever in the last life did all the work,
so I could sit down to this feast of rhymes and kisses,
long singing lines and ecstasy.

Love poets are the worst of thieves,
after Ovid everybody's borrowing,
except, perhaps, Novalis, whose
words were from cloistered grieving.

Novalis loved his bride nobly.
She was so angelic no one cared she was a child.
When she was ill he studied medicine to cure her,
not well enough, nor was there time.
His calendar became the record of his grief for the
one thousand four-hundred thirty-one days till he died.

A cabinet holds my old calendar books.
Stacked, they are a weight of evidence
against my ability, to find or fashion,
that extraordinary line of love.

GHOSTS OF POETRY

When you accept
you're at the mercy of
your wildest speculations,
you have a chance.
You hold the necessary pen,
the brooding posture, but
poems write themselves–
dreams are non-negotiable–
as hopes blossom,
the way ghosts
gather in the evening
to decide
to chastise us
or set us free.

THE WARRIOR'S TRAJECTORY

Scurrilous, the slaughter of innocents,
Respecting the life and death of only their own.
But the Vikings had this part of it right–
Put the body on a well-carved boat.
Drape it on a bed of rare sandalwood.
In his hand place the thing he loved most.
At sunset on a still, somber day,
Push the boat from the shore.
Loose flaming arrows into the wood.
Stand in hawk-like honor while it burns.
Watch while the boat goes, slowly,
Where it's going.

SHADOWED LIGHT

Sometimes she'd take my hand,
walk where, through a patch of trees,
we could see the moon trafficking in solitude.
And it was ours–
no clouds moving,
in its appetite outshining the sky.
And she, with an uncanny link to it,
telling me about–
the changing shapes, colors,
its pull on the waters of earth,
topography,
the rock-reflected light,
all I wanted to know about
darkness, the risk of eclipse, closing the distance.
It seemed almost physical,
the intensity of feeling,
the spectral shadowed light
coming from the moon,
each other.

ENDLESS FORMS MOST BEAUTIFUL

"Never suppose the atoms had a plan"
Lucretius 94-49 B.C.E.

There are seven vertebrae in the neck of a giraffe,
(stretched for the higher, sweeter leaves)
and seven in the human, whales, all mammals.
The Hox genes tell them to develop differently.

Overwhelming is the evidence that all animals:
birds, beetles, basques, worms, welsh, wolverines,
emerged from a few, primitive bacterium.
Darwin was right about molecular descent.

Only eight genes out of twenty-five thousand
demarcate the difference of fruit fly and fish.
What a construing invention is the eye! Is it plausible
that *mind* could be thought of before it came to be?

We can marvel at the cunning, patient strategy
and still be stunned, that the ravishingly elegant,
random, mutating process at hand,
produced Madame Curie, Akhmatova and Chopin.

THE REAL FUNERAL

When the suits and the dresses and the preachers went away,
we had the real funeral, my brother and I sitting in the gravel
of a town we'd shaken off long ago.

We got there just as Fatboy and his gravedigger friends
were finishing their job. They were sweeping around their
newest grave, the place that was our father's last one.

They didn't seem surprised that we came back.
One man drove by and said, "Your daddy was a good one,"
but soon had the respect to go away.

In the silence made heavy by our grief, my brother finally said,
"Dad, I'm gay." I said, "Mother, I didn't love you, but you
had my respect," two long-suppressed benedictions.

We wondered aloud how far apart they were, so Fatboy
measured, told us twenty-one inches. It seemed about right.
The gravel, the grave and Fatboy in an Alabama town.

When they were ready to leave, Fatboy turned to tell us,
"Think of it like putting a coat in the closet."
It was the best thing anybody said that day.

We stayed until we both felt calm begin to spread,
then we walked back toward the useless, emptying house.
That was the way we closed the door.

INFIDELITY

In love,
while all is fair, not all is retrievable.
There is an inequality of consequence,
the way a very small bird,
can halt such a large thing as silence.

Unfaithfulness
can serrate a braid of many years.
Like crystal shattering instantly,
its repair far from certain,
and, even then, certainly imperfect.

ONE TURN TO ARKANSAS

Had I made a right turn,
I might have been in Arkansas,
sitting on a bench having a picnic,
the first one of spring,
by the Arkansas River that
spindles through Little Rock,
talking with a woman
I used to date in college, who,
when I called to tell her I was coming,
ran out to get some Cabernet and camembert,
put on a flower print dress
that showed her grown up body
to splendid advantage, and
having certain randy memories,
was hoping I had more on my mind
than a day trip.
But I turned left,
don't ask me why,
the void has no inner sense,
and here I am at Stop'N Go,
eating a day-old donut,
filling the car with gas
on the way to a ballgame, alone.
All these roads:
curved, steep, unpredictable,
and looking at the ones gone over–
the choices,
extravagantly strange.

AN ALTERED PERSPECTIVE

In a fable of reverse engineering,
if you could, would you—
knowing all you know now—
choose not to be born?
Avoiding suffering, but never having seen Machupicchu,
not knowing love, in exchange for never losing it,
lacking wonder, for the lack of certainty,
never hearing Mozart, but not enduring the empty silence afterward.

Escaping the wretched injustice of the world,
but missing—
an ethereal day on Annapurna,
all is silent, white,
nowhere is there pain, impurity,
when in the distance
a snow leopard, or the holy
briefly moved into sight.

TOBIAS SMOLLETT

The way I won that fascinating woman,
was waking up startled in the stupored night

declaring, with all faculties otherwise intact,
"Tobias Smollett lives." It was the first time

she told me that she loved me, ravenously
laughing, having looked, she said,

with her skewed, side-ways eyes for a man
that crazy-smart all her grown-up life.

I said to a friend once, referring to my
spotty love career, "Why do I always

attract troubled women," to which she,
smirking like a west-coast guru, replied,

"Why do you always seek them out?"
Perhaps it's no coincidence we met

in Santa Barbara, a Spanish, white-washed town
of salmon-colored houses, lavish with

stargazers, eucalyptus, bougainvillea,
where they claim so many lousy days in paradise,

balanced as it is on the hemisphere's most unstable,
deep-running, ready-to-erupt fault line.

THE MISSING SUM OF INTEGERS

Every form of life is a usable channel– dividing, copying,
   proliferating, till exhausted, sloughed away.
   Dust is time's favored verb.

Nature hammers all through the arbiters of chance and
   survival. What splendor lost– only one percent of
   species have survived?

How could one imagine an ostrich, the ponderous beauty
   of rhinoceros, an orchid, a singing whale,
   snails shooting darts of love?

Of that flow we are. Complicated by the invasive whirlwind
   of symbols and history. Knowing, but not enough–
   linchpin of mastery and torment.

Two constituent worlds– mind and thing, the beast we were,
   in rarefied clothing. And all these absences, not before seen,
   long epiphanies of absence.

Earth flies through space at one hundred thousand miles
   per hour. And we don't notice it. How agreeable,
   this getting used to anything.

Anything except the absences– of a sum to be made from
   the integers, a structure that may finally appear, of a plot
   emerging from the infinite ocean of time.

SEVEN TIBETAN MONKS

From Tibet to our museum
in saffron robes and sandals they arrived,
with dorjes, vajras, a hundred ancient thangkas,
their bodhisattvas winking from the halls,
where art's western canon usually hangs.

An odd tableaux– the city's social register,
fastidious, polite, and these mystic foreigners,
black residue of yak butter candles grimy
under their fingernails– staring at each other
across infinite divides.

The monks make a sand mandala,
painstakingly painting, placing thousands of grains,
a delicate replication of the world,
only to destroy it,
bearing witness to impermanence of things.

We live in a white tent,
then disappear in a river,
its black eye closing behind us,
our histories vanishing,
as if from prayer flags flapping in the wind.

The fragile mandala completed,
in the monks' tantra chanting–
mesmerizing voices–
the felt world arose, was streaming by,
thrumming its uncoiling, evanescent wonder.

I SEE THE HUMOR OF IT NOW

She could have made a fool
out of Solomon, Diogenes and Kant,
all in one day. She was that–

goddess– remarkable. Caneletto
would have laid down his brush
on the spot. And I was in a line

I didn't know the length of,
greedy for the excess, the mad
extravagance, as if I'd

wandered in a cave, found
grouchy old Catullus,
scribbling on his parchment,

and he handed me a note which said,
"The love of a beautiful woman
is more than the conquering of Spain."

But a poet's lines were useless
in light of her capricious disappearing.
I'll be bold and tell you: my heart,

once ravaged, is now cleaned out,
a place so empty
the universe itself couldn't fill it.

MIND IN ITS PROFUSION

Now this world, this accumulated memory,
Instructive to parse its obbligato,
Call what can be beckoned to the surface.

On a mountainside, death is not philosophy.
The escape from time which her love always was.
A baton that coaxed the sorrow of Brahms' Requiem.
Beauty when it owned me, which was every time.

The rank profusion of the mind, recurring.
If a thing has disappeared, was it there? Where?
Am I the wind or the wall it blows against?
I choose the wind for the freedom of wandering.

On some night when stars make no sound,
While it lasts, they will sense passing by,
My lessened body, and its vapor trail of memory.

IF WE COULD TELL COPERNICUS

When I was young we were taught
there were *four billion* galaxies–
each with their own four billion stars,
plus the planetary systems, of which
earth is a minor, blue, watery example.

The lonely Hubble telescope revised the number
upward to *four hundred billion* galaxies,
each containing trillions of stars,
a million times larger than the earth,
the galaxies rapidly receding from each other.

As outlandish as Zeus or Zoroaster,
we think that before the *big bang,*
matter was all so densely compressed,
it was the size of a major league baseball,
created by a quantum fluctuation in the vacuum.

As a crow cannot consider a cloudburst, only
flies from the rain– our minds not yet equipped,
to grasp this extravagance and tittle,
though its vastness scribes the arc of our wonder
and frames our spirits' inclination.

PRAISE BEAUTY

You may say whatever polite thing you wish.
It was her beauty I most wanted, always.
I endured more rainy days, than fell on

All of Asia, for the times when the sun,
Burst across her profile, heaven sent scrambling
To preserve its reputation as paradise.

In all directions there is ugliness, suffering,
Loss. But by mercy of the gods, our
Eye is apprehended by the beautiful.

For this mute invocation, beauty should be
Closely observed and praised. And, to me,
She is its dark hush, its avalanche.

BECKETT'S LAST SILENCE

They asked where to lay him,
his having said, "I'm done."
"By Suzanne," he told them,
"she came back for me," referring
to the Paris street thief who
stabbed and left him dying.
His agate-spare mind,
his cowlick recalcitrant,
this maestro of the absurd,
who thought unhappiness was folly,
at the end still got his rugby scores,
drank his Bushmills daily,
signed copies, with agonizing effort,
of an Irish compendium,
thirteen days before he died
(while singing childhood hymns).
His falcon eyes seeing all he'd seen,
the search for the right kind
of empty silence ended.
Finding it, he gestured
by lying down, in the dust, still,
next to her.

A NOTE FROM NIETZSCHE TO FREUD

Yes, I heard
you helped Mahler
find the memories
oddly piping
in his music.
What makes
you think
you could
fix me?
Surely you understand
what ails me
has never been
subject
to tinkering.
The cure
for this angst
is another 10th Symphony
that doesn't
exist.

II

"It is impossible to fight with what the soul has chosen."

STEFAN ZEROMSKI

Artist: Stuart Gentling

PYTHIA

All we have is a portion of her face
in bronze. Perhaps the statue fell
or was sold as scrap
for the Peloponnesian war.
From what remains you can tell:
her eyes were pellucid,
the cut of her chin, noble, Athenian.
If she was lovely we can't know,
nor how gentle her voice,
nor whether when the wind took her hair,
it's fluttering could be seen by ships
returning in triumph from Troy.
Recalling another face lost to me,
reluctantly, I touch the relic–
she now added to the other one–
having even less of her
in front of me to look at,
but, nonetheless,
as if in bronze,
remembered.

THE GRAYING MOON

When I consider that the moon
followed me over six continents,
through days of desperation
and ones that gleamed like fire,
as I know its craters and dried streams,
surely it should know me by now.

Some nights it shines
with an outrageous brightness–
others, a pale, thin crescent,
untroubled that the sun's burning lessens.

The wandering has finally brought me here–
the moon complicit,
sharing the grayness
growing within me–
desire more rampant
than my ability to fill it.

The blue spinning planet I have circled,
one continent left to pitch a tent,
the moon hanging rock-like, waiting to go with me,
neither of us yet out of light.

RUSSIAN IRONY

I had lunch with Mischa, a Russian émigré, who raised
a vodka in his favorite Russian toast, "To the success of
our impossible task." Among the madness of 30 million

quick-firing deaths– his father and his uncle, the famous
General Kerensky. Death and fear forestall revolution.
In the purge of '37, pregnant women were not killed,

he and his mother lived, born with genes of a samizdat
writer. He and Brodsky became good friends– there is
a picture together in the snow of Arkhangelsk.

They were threatened by an agent whose forehead had
a port wine stain. They remembered an enigmatic smile.
Now, Mischa is a U.S. publisher, who translates books,

Russian and English, who received an order, for thirty
copies in Russian, of A. A. Milne's, *Winnie the Pooh*,
needed by a lady named Bush, as gifts for the Putins

in Moscow. In a poem titled, "So," Christopher Robin says,
"round about and round about I go." He filled the order.
Russian poetry and irony are almost impossible to translate.

THE MUSEUM OF LOVE

We've got museums for automobiles and circuses,
why not one for love? To commemorate
the unrelenting outbreak of passion, to present

the Cleopatra awards for ecstasy. Down this hall–
bliss. Over there– long suffering. Around the corner:
options, alternatives. The chapel in honor of

Heloise and Abelard. A vestibule for pre-nuptial
agreements, a lock-down for lawyers of divorce,
the Board undecided what to do about courtesans.

The Kama Sutra has a special room, as does poetry:
Yeats, Shelley, Sappho, Ovid, and Shakespeare.
A font for alms to honor unrequited love.

What will a common woman see when she comes
here, and what will a common man feel? A secret
similar to saying "God" in a cathedral, so powerful

only a small word could express it. A mystery
as beautiful as a body fiercely held, seldom truly had–
only rarely– honored, in this museum.

PLANETARY SONG

Pluck a string of any size.
Cut another exactly half its length.
It sounds the octave of the chord.

The gargantuan moaning of a black hole,
A B^b, fifty seven octaves below middle "C"–
The "music of the spheres" of Pythagoras.

Unheard until the hearer appeared.
The flute and the drum before speech.
Mozart notating the ineffable.

Light, like hate, expands in all directions.
Sound is more like love, requires atmosphere,
In this case, gravity's molecules to pass through.

Deep-time travelers, unfamiliar with song,
When entering the Milky Way galaxy,
Find a curiosity widely remarked upon.

That from a planet called Earth can be heard–
Life being hammered into music, murmuring,
Wherever there are tenements of sound.

SOLO

Theft of words–
was it Nixon's secretary
erasing the tape,
a mischievous angel,
a many-armed invidious octopus,
who stole the directory,
blurred the blueprint as if rubbed against slate–
the Oracle at Delphi mute as stone,
no place cards on any of the tables,
the whorl of stars yielding nothing but light–
if I could find the heavy book, I'd read it.
The blind, Braille life we lead,
feeling our way, like the
shadowy lurching of the trilobite, or
the pianist's imperious nod to the saxophone–
no written music, four chords–
you're on.

THE DIVORCE

Has anyone seen
the death of a river
from natural causes?
Usually the reason is
an intervention like a dam,
or some other change in topography.
On occasion,
discharges of effluent
have rendered the water unusable.
I suppose
it could just stop raining.
Then,
like our parting,
slowly the dying
would wind down
following the river bed,
for miles in the distance,
for years.

DARK ENERGY

Despite appearances,
there is no nothingness in space.

Dark energy constitutes
seventy percent of all that is.
Einstein was right, though
he thought it an egregious error.

Whatever it turns out to be,
it restrains the infinitely expanding universe,
hurtling toward the outer edge in all directions,
which otherwise would tear itself apart.

It instructs gravity
to operate within its proper sphere.
It is the latest piety–
unseen, indescribable, without current proof.

Because it accounts for what we actually see,
we believe it's out there,
holding things together
keeping the cosmos in balance,

moving through the atoms which comprise us,
having an effect we can calculate.
Perhaps the eternity we've looked for,
the most recent description of a god.

THE IMMENSE EXPECTATIONS OF SPRING

Two tree swallows occupy the tiny house
on the deck by the window where I write in Oregon.
Having laid in twigs and netting,
several times a day for several days
she dangles on the slanted roof
as he circles by.
A sideways glance confirms it's him,
she spread her tail wings
and he enters–
one or two attempts before he falls away,
not being a hummingbird
who can, ghost-like, suspend himself in air–
his hunger persistent,
after a tight, keening arc
she allows him back,
till today, it seems it's finished.
They sit side by side,
and, while he guards,
dueling with a stellar jay four times his size,
she disappears into the nest–
more intent than any machinery–
in their natural, relentless continuing.

ABSENCE OF BIRDS

You don't actually hear
the absence of birds.
You hear the foot crunch
on the accumulating snow,
the absence just registers,
the silence eerily compounded.

As the emptiness that occupies
the closed, forgotten place–
gnawed out by love-
can leap up at remembering
a laugh, a scent,
a woman's soft touch.

And,
after a moment
of shameless happiness,
you go on,
each step marking
the darkening snow.

A FEW POEMS

An epigram,
in its Greek derivation,
means a scratching on stone–
the way the years, on me,
have etched their tokens and signs.
You can see the chiseling
by opening a vein
and watching weathered words
tumble out.

IN SEARCH OF SOCRATES

For hundreds of years, they couldn't find the prison
that executed Socrates– gadfly, obstreperous, corrupter
of youth, over-large head caused by the size of his doubts.
They dug all over the Agora, until an archaeologist surmised,
erosion from the hill of the Acropolis might have covered it
in shame. It was found near the road to Pireaus and the sea,
where Crito begged Socrates to escape, Athens having
left the doors open overnight. Philosophers from Princeton
verified the site. Patterns of the floors cross-referenced to
the Dialogues, they found it about right. I took a pilgrimage
to see the stones. It was winter. Wild dogs were chasing
what they could. A few couples walked beside the Temple
of Apollo, the Monument of Eponymous Heroes, the
bulletin board where Meletus tacked his fatal allegations.
Pavlos had given me the philosophers' report. I touched
every stone. Not that wisdom might rub off on me–
I don't have the words to parry with Plato, nor the courage
to rail against the unjust state. Only to honor in this
anti-cathedral, a life well used, in the rigorous, examined,
authentic-to-the-death pursuit of truth.

HALF A HAPPINESS

Like a shadow's imaginary kiss,
or like dark matter,
unseen, but surely there,
my mind conjures you, still.

On Catherine's white marble stairs,
now the grand entrance to the Hermitage,
unbidden you appeared by the pink-veined balustrade,
half a happiness.

I thought I saw you just below the landing,
stole on your shoulder as once in a lesser hall,
where, right or left, you must choose
which entryway for beauty to come upon beauty.

When the shadow-dream ended,
it was mine to choose,
which images to carry, descending,
into the brightened, common world.

CURFEW

I am atoms strung together,
brief gathering,
shimmer of molecules,
a fleeting voice rented with
an indifferent curfew.
Joys, sorrows–
a thrum of butterflies,
my cleaving–
a river's fingernails grasping at the bank–
what a whetstone pain is.

But I am atoms
imbued with curiosity,
particles erupting in words, song,
who courted wonder,
who loved
and believed
in unsayable things,
who will disappear
with bristling defiance
and calm gratitude.

THE PROBLEM IS THE WHALES

The problem is the whales.
And why they beach themselves.
And why we are helpless as their weight crushes them.
And why their eyes are so knowing.
Like some of us,
they want to be through with it,
the senseless, endless swimming.
Maybe they've been chosen,
(like the Druid prince killed three times
to keep the Romans from invading Ireland)
representatives of sentient beings, sent to ask
that we stop murdering them.
Or, something gone wrong in the mechanism,
so acutely wound it is subject to malfunction,
disoriented, causing a fatal turn.
Or, that they've lumbered those lugubrious depths,
their dark sunk cities,
dreamed of a brightening paradise of air,
and were willing to risk everything
to get there.

DIFFERENCES

The difference between
looking at a mountain in the distance,
and standing on its peak,

is the difference between
attending a seminar on beauty, and
watching the loved one emerge from the ocean,

wet hair, suit clinging,
tenderness rising from her eyes,
surefooted,

walking straight toward me,
as if a gift,
she and the water were offering.

WHAT HEAVEN WE CAN HAVE

Odd, such unlikely consonance–
The rhythmic rumbling of frogs around the pond,
The low-throated humming of the monks of Drepung–
Each pierce the night like giant bassoons.

An intake of breath producing endless repetition,
The rising and falling of the guttural tone,
Searching, sounding for the resonance
Embedded at the deep, molten core.

As we sometimes can hold,
Everything in balance for a luminous moment,
Which then drifts away,
But is often remembered,
As what heaven we can have.

THE HEART ATTACK

The pulsing red muscle has a scar on the back—
difficult to see, stretched against the diaphragm,
an artifact, proof of an event. The interview begins,
"Do you remember a night of wrenching pain?"

Numb, I hear myself recounting
the Lo-Muthang climb four years ago—
(while the Kafka gene smirks, blames existentialism,
the romantic gene argues
that woman's mark cannot be irradiated)
when I had to stop, turn back, come down.

These endings all begin the same way: calm
empathy, good advice, then, alone with the news.
I pay at the counter, walk outside, wonder if a
scar has weight, everything suddenly heavier.

Strange for a stoic to delay a date with facts,
but I thought of Shelley's heart—
when Shelley in a storm, overturned his boat,
when Byron burned the body on the shore,
and reached in for the heart
which no flame but his words could engulf.

THE HELL AWAITING GIOVANNI

Is there an abacus of the heart? There is a need
from time to time, for an accounting. For example.
Love's misfortunes can cause severe withdrawal,
as if behind the walls surrounding Florence.
Protected. Secure. (The third wall lasted
seven-hundred years). But if the siege of pain
is not soon lifted, the heart will atrophy. And
you'd look in vain for someone to surrender to.

Or, an opposite case. Twice is half as innocent
as once. The fourth or seventh time may have
special circumstance. The twelfth and fifteenth,
more of dark need than gladness. After that,
decadent descent, banished from delight,
what irony— despising the object of desire.
Why do you imagine Donatello's Magdelena is crying?
Because the purity of Florence is now only a memory.

THE BLUE HERON, JUSTIFIED

The blue heron, with inordinate grace, flew
down in quietness, between the river willow
and the waterfall, posed by the water as if
another statue, perched on bamboo. With
crafted motion, struck and swallowed an
iridescent koi from my pond– feathered
instrument of death, wing-span enormous,
lifting, banked, elevated out of sight. It's not
just a matter of perspective. *We've a right
to what we create*, says the analytical mind.
Not so fast, says the goddess, *look how
fragile is your wrist*. Beauty has nine ways
of withering, love plumes, then is wrenched
away, into the flux. The intrinsic force,
capricious, a juggernaut, lurches on.
Assertion or denial makes no difference.
All we can do is never stop saying yes.

A PALPABLE LIGHT

Nowhere are there such degrees of blueness
or green, as in Antarctica's waters, hollow-winged
albatross gliding above the blatant ice.

Silence broken by the humpback's breaching,
waddling penguins offer pebbles to their mates,
petrel choirs singing with echoing tongues.

The cannon crack of an ice-mound's calving–
glaciers scattered like a white Stonehenge,
cormorants criss-crossing the caldera.

Time's measures missing, the moon's brightness
falling from the air, nothing in the moment, no
economy, kings, away from the palaces of ruin.

Guest of this grandeur– found by the palpable light–
I sail in the wilderness of natural being,
past myth into seeing– earth's phosphorescent night.

ANOTHER YEAR

If words were a latchkey,
I'd have been behind that door for years,
under the roof
where the rightness was ubiquitous,
in a room with a candle,
you, blind to me in all but your body.
Who knows what dusty grievances
the year shook away,
the way the last notes of Mahler fade.
I'll live on the back stairs
until you explain,
what heart could be impervious
to words, singing,
to the way when on both of us
the perfect light gambols
over all the infinite world.

THE NECESSITY OF DECEMBER

In the endless processions in the afterlife, billions
of people, back to the Cro-Magnon, waiting to interview
the deities, with questions we could never get the answers to.
I'd choose the shorter lines- to speak to Emily Dickinson,
Voltaire, or the enigmatic Genghis Khan. For that, I wouldn't
mind waiting. What do we have, after all, but time?

We used to think, with foreboding, in this other life, when
death would arrive in Act V, that all our lassitude- the
unkempt roaming of our lives- could not have a meaningful
shape if not brought to conclusion, everything framed by the
boundary parentheses. What virtuosity we thought, to force all
the pieces to fuse into a whole, by marking a beginning and end.

GROWING INTO POETRY

I have studied beauty in Vermeer, the way he uses light,
   the way it streams through the window, falls upon
   the table, floor and the woman who waits to be immersed.

But I've seldom seen beauty like the eyes of a nine-year-old
   child, growing into poetry. By keen seeing, awakening
   a power to describe, her rapt face discovering–

The way she names the world can give delight.
   I imagine her in fifteen years, a woman,
   standing under blinking stars, rain plastering her

Clothes, her body's silhouette flung obvious,
   feeling by the night's reflected light, something
   mysterious, almost divine, a discontinuity

Within her, and in fateful exuberance,
   searching for stilts, to keep that lucid moment
   hovering in air, as long as her balance and reach will allow.

Then it settles, the disappearing light having whispered–
   that words and the heft of her days are malleable,
   can be invented, polished, engraved.

WHITE NIGHTS

The surreal white nights of St. Petersburg,
night and day plaited,
cannot be told apart,
seamless ones like we could never find.

I think of you and all those bright days,
pulled from my shoulder now
like small barbs of happiness.
Those nights so holy we knew we'd been painted.

Artists, highly sensitive, overreact,
faster than photons disconnect, attract.
Yes, we drank the wine of astonishment,
but what we swallowed was our own brilliance.

Halfway round the world, your letter in my hand–
we are continents slowly edging back–
the map in need of correction, in need of the beauty
of undivided days, wandering our parcel of heaven.

ALONENESS

In the brutal force
of solitude,
surrounded by a
long gray happening,
being alone affects the eye–
it looks less lovingly at everything,
it dulls the ear–
shrinks the range of sound,
stills the tongue–
so little to proclaim,
it reduces the heart–
less used, less required.
I know–
as if a ghost
has taken residence in my senses,
and neither of us can find
an open window or an unlocked door.

AN INTRODUCTION TO THE SPIRIT

Concentrate, said the poet,
it is we who must articulate the night.
Dark veined enough, I demurred,
described what I saw in plain sight.
On the savannah of Ngorongoro, if you
see the acacia trained by the wind as a bonsai,
you miss the history of trees. How to be spare,
get all the way through to the maw.
Show me the spirit of the thing, said the skeptic.

I say, an orca breaches for the joy of it.
The round-tabled knights, their intended purity.
The strict, selfless code of the samurai.
Ancient Athens, the Althing, Alhambra.
A dolphin pulls a human from the sea.
Not from religion or empire which oppress,
but the silence from which bursts poetry.
A small planet struggles up to language,
perilous love, and liquid song.

THE JOYFUL ENTOMOLOGIST

She knew all my faults
  dissected them
  like a joyful entomologist.

Rubbing the beetle's belly
  till I coughed up every crime,

Pulling off each leg
  one by painful one,

Clipping wings with the
  scissors of her grievances,

carefully hoarded, against
  the chance of low supply.

The results of her research:
  a dead bug is better than a live one.

A master of her craft,
  she operates now,
  fortunately for me
  on someone else.

EXISTENTIALISM

None of us
were consulted
regarding our existence.

Nonetheless,
compelled,
we make a thing of it.

Life is
in our hands, is
ours to construct.

Except the final
exclamation point,
which will be provided.

THE EMPTY AEGEAN

No wonder there were
so many gods in the Aegean,
the world's too mad for only one.

Intent on a fully human world,
we took back their powers,
from Olympus exiling them to libraries.

Time revises our mythologies,
Brodsky wrote nativity poems, what
Nietzsche destroyed, Seferis depended on.

Myth is borrowed for its meaning,
lending our stories a scaffolding,
so our sentences don't crumble into silence.

But justice often comes too late in these stories–
too late to learn– mortality's portal
is the catalyst of knowledge.

All death is absence, and when the gods die,
the void wants filling–
an indwelling impulse, an inquietude–

which started our dancing, drumming,
writing in rhyme, our breaking into
sad, defiant song.

PASSION

The morning after the first time together,
I found a note, folded by the orange juice.
"Don't tell me you love me if you don't."
    She was Cuban.
    Among other things,
    her passion was pure tobacco leaf,
    fragrant smoke, slow, low-burning.
    Her father was a freedom fighter,
    who either did or didn't, hide on a bridge,
    and attack, by himself, a Cuban boat.
I was scrupulously careful in everything I said after that.

A CONSOLATION

Mystery and magic in the skies
no astronomy can weaken–
Neanderthal to the blood of Inca,
even yesterday.
Older and bigger than we thought–
the Hubble constant was understated–
the universe is 180 billion light-years wide.
We *are* dust of stars,
rain of their explosions,
drawn to the origin of light.
Compelled to look upward,
appeal to, travel toward,
in ancient argument with night.
Bound in time,
we yearn to escape it,
our small deaths mirroring
their vast ones–
those radiant rebirths in which
our role is less grand
than our knowing makes us hope,
but playing the only speaking part.

WHERE BEAUTY BEGINS

Cold descended on the land.
For over thirty years, a mini ice-age,
especially around Cremona.
Children and the elderly died from the freeze.
Plants and trees went dormant,
stressed, couldn't push leaves.
Barrenness spread like ether.
Obsessed, Stradivarius persisted–
hauled the wood, cut, scraped, shaped,
used pine sap, resins, glues, horsehair–
the formula forgotten, abandoned by his sons.
After many years the violins
began to sing with an unearthly rapture,
whispering a pain, a persistent desire,
a sweetness beyond human artifice.
The wood had become immaculate,
as if torn from the mouth of our yearning,
warming, still, the cold around us.

POET IN RIGHT FIELD

They put me in right field
where I'd do the least damage,
they hoped.

It was a huge game. The other
team's first baseman had a brother
who was in the N. F. L.

Somebody hadn't shown up.
What was I, twelve? Scared as a calf in a
river, trying not to show it.

Everybody parked their pick-ups
pointed to the field so the headlights
let us see the bases.

Their pitcher threw
the ball too fast, I couldn't hit it.
My team didn't care.

The only thing that mattered
was the shot hit toward me with a
man on third in the ninth.

I ran it down, threw it on the
slanted curve, hard as I could– it got there
just before the runner.

The atta-boy pummeling was like a
new dog and Christmas- the first time
scrambling over puberty.

In the eighth inning now I use pad, pen,
table, and walls to keep the words in.
Making as few errors as I can.

Circling the bases with that unfettered feeling,
searching for the sweet curving whirr,
on fields less joyous, but satisfying and serene.

THE ONLY SHADOW ON THE MOUNTAIN

I climb in the silence,
the faultless mountains of Tibet.
Yet all I want to do,
after all these years,
is retrieve the sandal
you left on the beach,
the night we made love
at the gulf of Pensacola.

Why did we exchange
desire for memory?
What do you think of
as you unlock
the clasp of your pearls?
How high will this
shadow go with me,
so far from any sand?

SWANS IN TEXAS

The swans liked April better than August,
  summer bleached their feathers really white,
  spread by their preening on the ground, soft arrows.

The pecking order was easily established,
  themselves, the wood ducks, everyone else,
  no herons. Explained like the 5 o'clock news.

We trapped raccoons to keep them from the eggs,
  but another would assume the territory,
  just as no beautiful woman is alone very long.

The swans bathed in the fountain that came on at night.
  They responded to our attention, though self-possessed,
  as if the origin of their grace couldn't be talked about.

They were agitated only when they tried to fly,
  needing fifty feet to start, they had thirty-five,
  stopped short, it seemed they were practicing.

Eyes to see it beautiful, made it so– the
  blurring of Monet, a December baby in a
  Christmas sock, an elf sitting on the edge of irony.

PHYSICS OF THE AIR

Every time I walk outside,
the ravens start their ribald screaming,
distempered viceroys of the sky,
cruising the streets of the high tossed branches,
like children squabbling in their aerie of toys,
threatening, banked turns when I appear.

They didn't build the pond, plant the dogwood–
from which they haughtily accuse–
or the crossvine, which has covered the pergola,
beneath which a bench was placed
for anyone to sit on a lanky afternoon so their
breathing would slow down from tranquility.

Perhaps a territorial compromise–
since they are free to climb against gravity,
to explore the physics of the air
as if death doesn't happen up there–
I'll give what we know an alphabet,
they'll be its black, whirling signature.

THE EPIC OF GILGAMESH

I stare at stars that stare at me,
space-washed white, the light I see—
thirteen billion years old—
the flare of the beginning not yet in sight.

Or stare at history's similar anomalies—
the law of phylogeny, each of us a summary of all that's been,
the trail of footprints starts in Africa, then Sumer, then the moon,
the billions of years required to finish the first sentences.

Wine is the pummeling of grapes,
a poem the mirage of uttered wonder,
a heart the held antiphony of gathering and loss,
a flower the becoming of its root.

And what of the scattered world itself?
If we stare at it long enough,
through our fogged theories,
back to the beginning in the flood of either myth,

will we ever see Gilgamesh or Eden,
a small signpost,
the first mailbox with key,
or at least,
an angel in the wind?

EPILOGUE

ACCIDENTAL HAPPINESS

I am not smarter than to write fragile
   hopes on the vellum of despair.
Like a cedar-waxwing drunk
   on laurel cherry leaves,
I've always stumbled into
   accidental happiness.

Rode out against feckless hate.
   Dreamed another planet's
Jewelry. Made a coat of many
   colors from a hair shirt. Foraged
For love on the plain of disasters.
   Put on the skin of all the earth.

In fact, I've assembled
   the city of a convoluted joy.
And now, body slowing, the soul
   avoiding corrosion, so far,
Am still fiercely grinning at its
   gradual, reluctant relinquishing.

NOTES

11   Light Year- the distance light travels in a vacuum in one terrestrial year- 5,878,422,164,161 miles. Therefore, the object cited in the poem is 470,273,773,132,880 miles long.

12   Two of Borges' favorite cities were Austin and Geneva, which he visited as he sensed the approach of the end of his life.

23   Hox genes function in patterning the body axis in most insects and animals. "Endless forms most beautiful," is a phrase from Darwin's, "The Origin of Species."

36   Mahler and Freud had a long-delayed (by Mahler) session. They met halfway, each coming by train. Freud wrote later that no patient worked harder to make progress in such a brief time.

41   True, some names changed.

53   A 2,000 year old body was recently found in a English peat bog. Research indicates it was a Druid prince ritually sacrificed to persuade the gods to prevent the Romans from invading Ireland. They didn't.

70   Referring to the note for page 11, the width of the universe is approximately 1,058,116 (+ 18 zeroes) miles wide.